HALLOWEEN COLORING BOOK

Thank you for choosing Ava Browne Coloring Books.
We strive to publish unique coloring books for all ages.

This coloring book contains double images, meaning you get to try different colors and shading for every page!!

If you found this coloring book enjoyable, please leave us a review.
Reviews help drive sales which allows us to make more coloring books.
Thank you and happy coloring!

This book includes a free digital copy that you can print out at home. For instructions and your access Code, please go to the last page.

Please vist www.avabrowne.com to see all of our books and to sign up for free coloring pages!

COLOR TEST PAGE

COLOR TEST PAGE

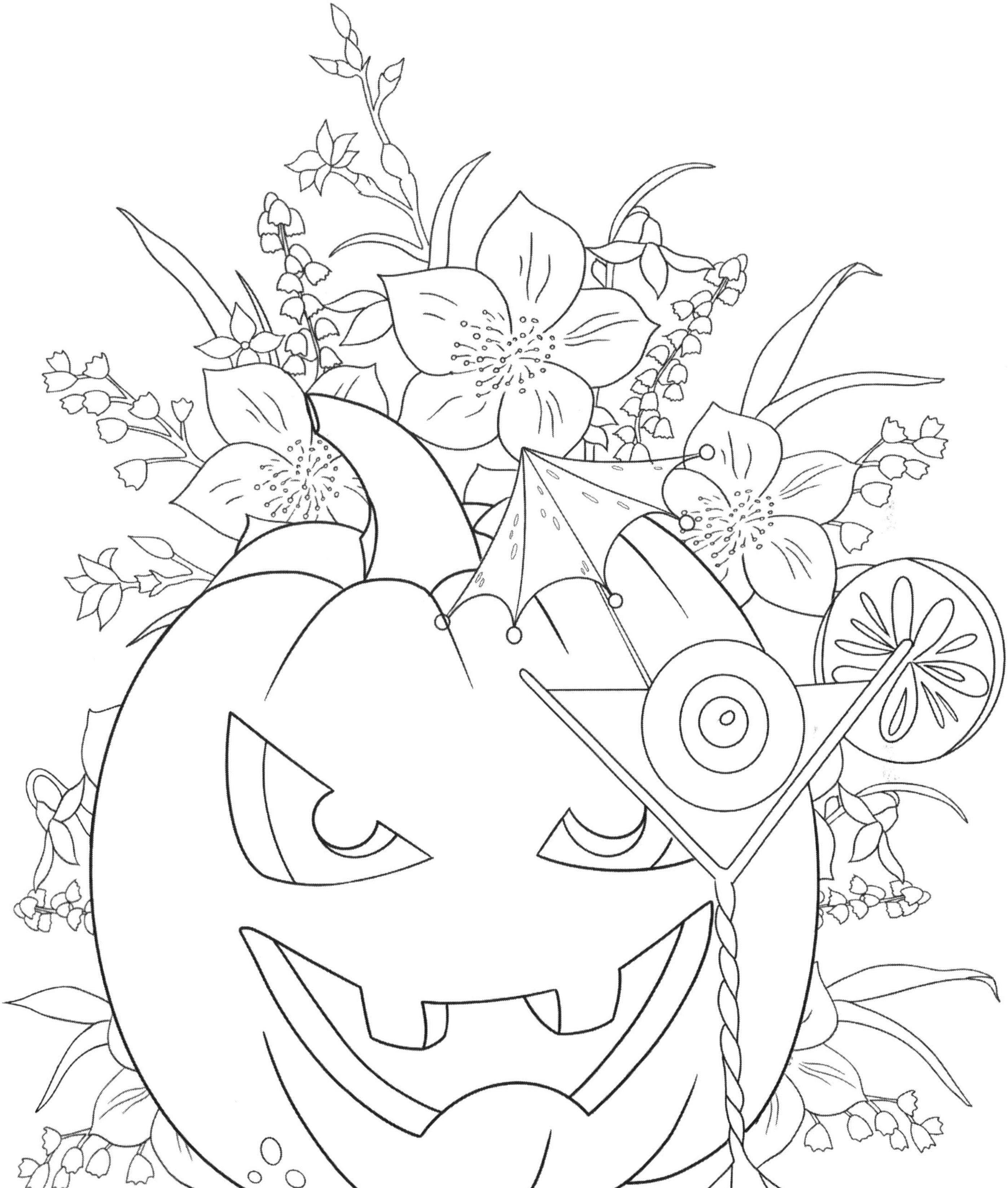

**Please visit
https://avabrowne.com/halloween-download/
to download your free digital copy.**

**Please consider subscribing to our newsletter, and
enter the password *k7tmuy2r* to access the file.
(All Lowercase)**